PLANETS

EARTH

Alexis Roumanis

www.av2books.com

LET'S READ
AV²
BY WEIGL™
ADDED VALUE • AUDIO VISUAL

AV² provides enriched content that supplements and complements this book. Weigl's AV² boo[k]
strive to create inspired learning and engage young minds in a total learning experience.

Your AV² Media Enhanced books come alive with...

Go to **www.av2books.com**,
and enter this book's
unique code.

BOOK CODE

Y774648

AV² by Weigl brings you media
enhanced books that support
active learning.

Audio
Listen to sections of
the book read aloud.

Video
Watch informative
video clips.

Embedded Weblinks
Gain additional information
for research.

Try This!
Complete activities and
hands-on experiments.

Key Words
Study vocabulary, and
complete a matching
word activity.

Quizzes
Test your knowledge.

Slide Show
View images and
captions, and prepare
a presentation.

... and much, much more!

Published by AV² by Weigl
350 5ᵗʰ Avenue, 59ᵗʰ Floor New York, NY 10118
Websites: www.av2books.com   www.weigl.com

Library of Congress Cataloging-in-Publication Data

Roumanis, Alexis, author.
 Earth / Alexis Roumanis.
     pages cm. -- (Planets)
 Includes index.
 ISBN 978-1-4896-3280-7 (hard cover : alk. paper) -- ISBN 978-1-4896-3281-4 (soft cover : alk. paper) -- ISBN 978-1-4896-3282-1 (single user ebook)
-- ISBN 978-1-4896-3283-8 (multi-user ebook)
 1. Earth (Planet)--Juvenile literature. I. Title.
 QB631.4.R68 2016
 525--dc23
                                 2014041516

Printed in the United States of America in Brainerd, Minnesota
1 2 3 4 5 6 7 8 9 0 19 18 17 16 15

022015
WEP081214

Project Coordinator: Katie Gillespie Art Director: Terry Paulhus

Weigl acknowledges Getty Images and iStock as the primary image suppliers for this title.

EARTH

CONTENTS

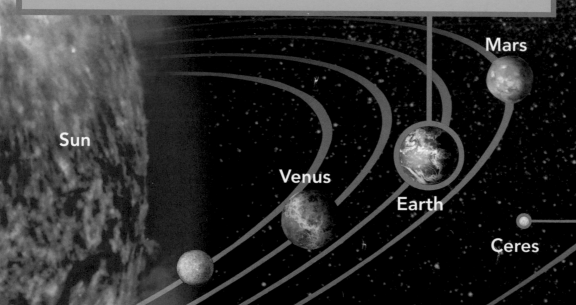

What Is Earth?

Earth is a planet. It moves in a path around the Sun. Earth is the third planet from the Sun.

Sun

Mercury

Venus

Earth

Mars

Ceres

Jupiter

Eris

Makemake

Haumea

Pluto

Neptune

Uranus

Saturn

Dwarf Planets

Dwarf planets are round objects that move around the Sun. Unlike planets, they share their part of space with other objects.

How Big Is Earth?

Earth is the fourth smallest planet in the solar system. It is almost the same size as Venus.

Earth

Venus

7

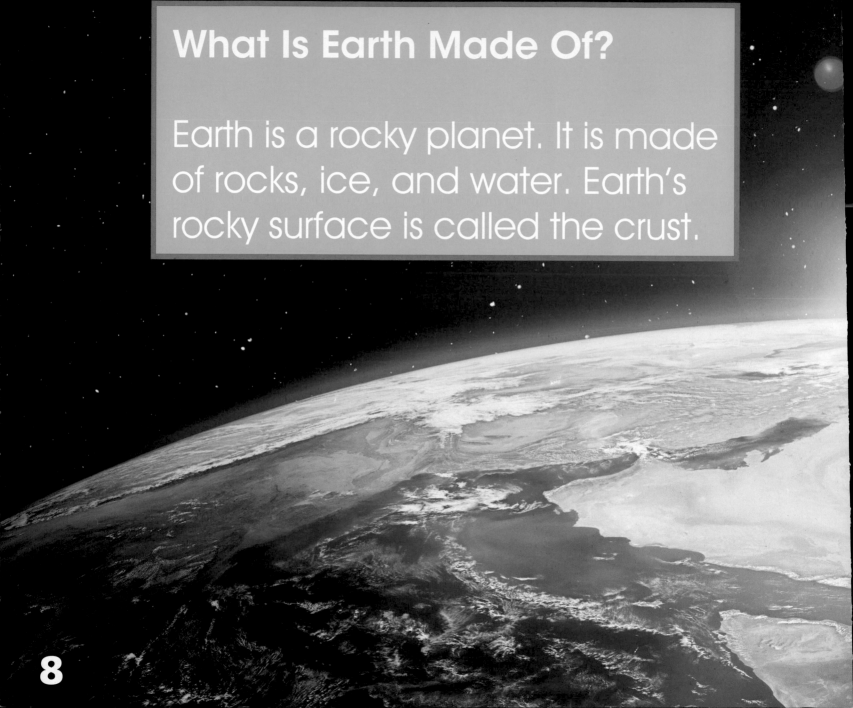

What Is Earth Made Of?

Earth is a rocky planet. It is made of rocks, ice, and water. Earth's rocky surface is called the crust.

9

10

What Does Earth Look Like?

Earth is the only known planet to have oceans of water. It is sometimes called the Blue Planet. Earth's oceans make it look blue.

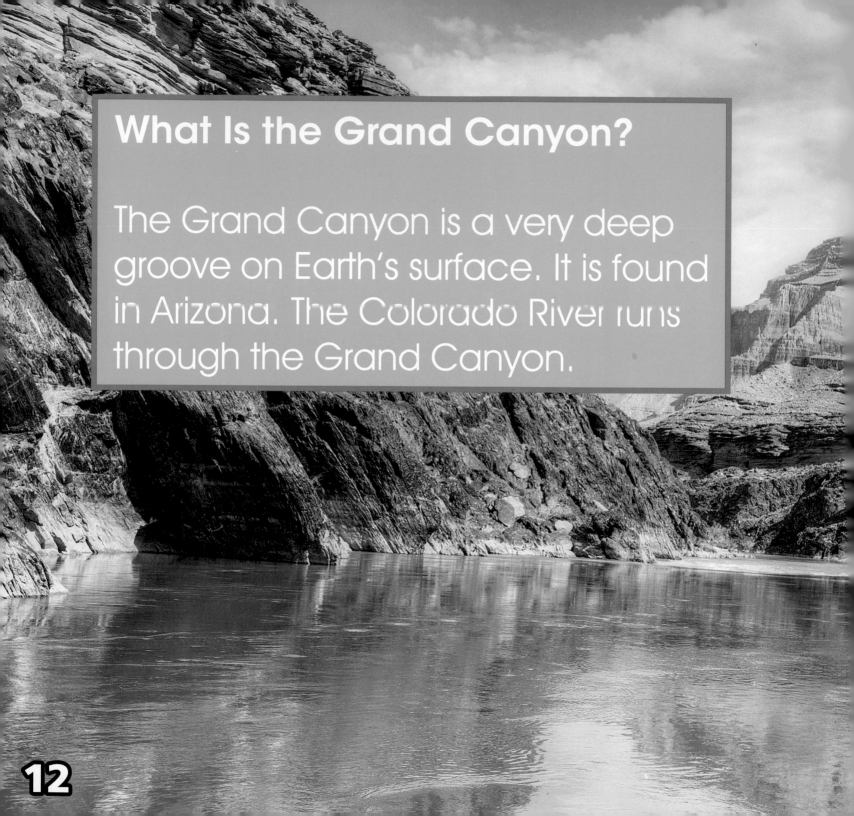

What Is the Grand Canyon?

The Grand Canyon is a very deep groove on Earth's surface. It is found in Arizona. The Colorado River runs through the Grand Canyon.

13

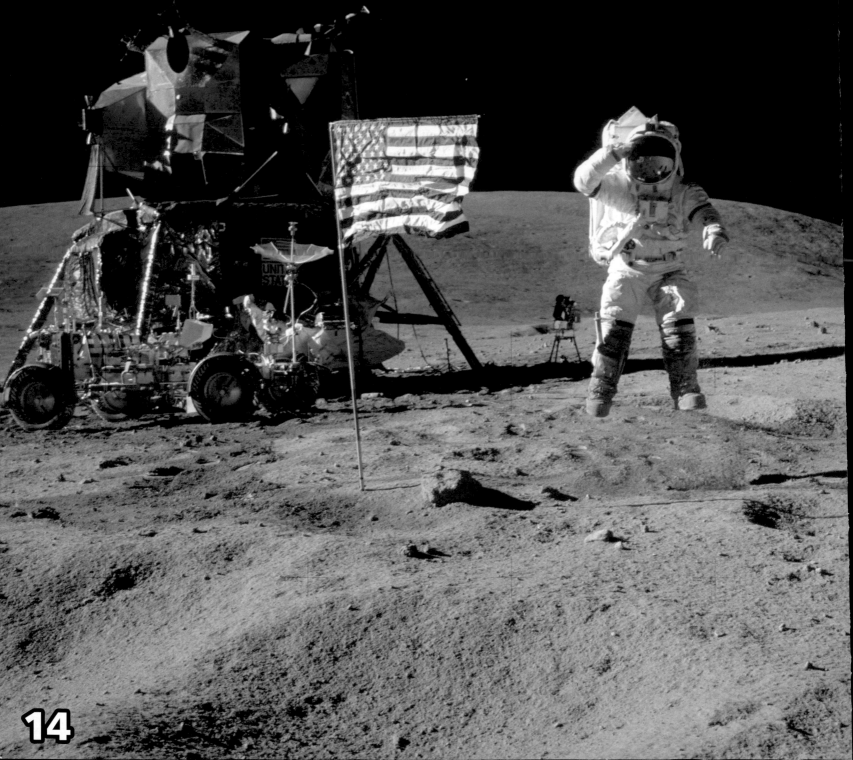

14

What Is Earth's Moon?

Earth has one moon. Some astronauts have traveled there. The first person walked on the Moon in 1969.

Earth

Moon

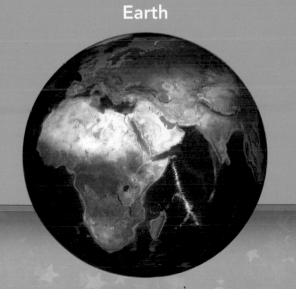

Who Discovered that Earth Is a Planet?

Copernicus discovered that Earth is a planet in the 1500s. He thought that Earth moves around the Sun.

18

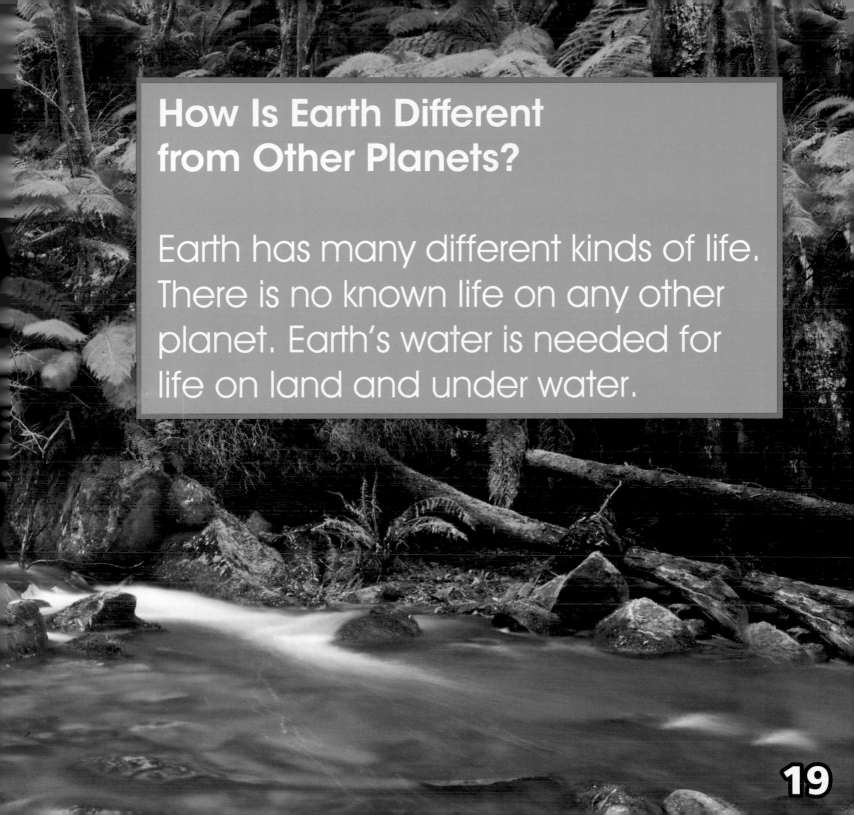

How Is Earth Different from Other Planets?

Earth has many different kinds of life. There is no known life on any other planet. Earth's water is needed for life on land and under water.

How Do We Learn about Earth Today?

A space station is a vehicle that moves around Earth. Astronauts live and work on the station. They study Earth from space.

EARTH FACTS

This page provides more detail about the interesting facts found in the book. They are intended to be used by adults as a learning support to help young readers round out their knowledge of each planet featured in the *Planets* series.

Pages 4–5

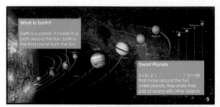

Earth is a planet. Planets are round objects that move around, or orbit, a star, with enough mass to clear smaller objects from their orbit. Earth's solar system has eight planets, five known dwarf planets, and many other space objects that all orbit the Sun. Earth is 93 million miles (150 million kilometers) from the Sun. It takes about 365 days for Earth to make one orbit around the Sun.

Pages 6–7

Earth is the fourth smallest planet in the solar system. It is only slightly larger than the planet Venus. Gravity is a force that pulls objects toward a planet's center. The force of gravity is almost the same on Venus as it is on Earth. A 100-pound (45-kilogram) object on Earth would weigh 91 pounds (41 kg) on Venus.

Pages 8–9

Earth is a rocky planet. Earth's surface is covered in about 75 percent water and 10 percent ice. The rest of the planet is covered in a rocky crust. Experts believe that Earth's center, called the core, is solid inside. This core is surrounded by a molten, or liquid, layer called the mantle.

Pages 10–11

Earth is the only known planet to have oceans of water. From space, Earth looks like a blue marble. It has white swirls and brown, yellow, green, and white areas. The blue parts of Earth are water. The white swirls are either clouds or areas that are covered in ice and snow. Brown, yellow, and green patches are land. Some farms and cities can even been seen from space.

The Grand Canyon is a very deep groove on Earth's surface. Many people consider it one of the seven natural wonders of the world. The Grand Canyon is around 6,000 feet (1,800 meters) deep and stretches 277 miles (446 km). Much of the Grand Canyon was formed by the Colorado River. The river has been eroding the canyon for millions of years.

Earth has one moon. Earth's moon is the fifth largest moon in the solar system. On average, it is approximately 238,855 miles (384,400 km) away from Earth. On July 20, 1969, American astronaut Neil Armstrong became the first person to step onto the Moon's surface. Since then, a total of 12 people have walked on the Moon.

Copernicus discovered that Earth is a planet in the 1500s. People once believed that the stars and other planets orbited Earth. In 1543, Nicolaus Copernicus wrote that Earth was not the center of the solar system. He argued that the Sun was actually at the center. In the early 1600s, the observations of Galileo Galilei supported this theory. The work of both men helped influence the thinking of all astronomers that followed.

Earth has many different kinds of life. Earth is unlike any other known planet in the solar system. It is made up of land, air, and water, which all work together to support life. Plants and animals are able to survive on Earth because it is in a habitable zone. This means that, unlike other planets, Earth is not too hot or too cold to support life.

A space station is a vehicle that moves around Earth. The *International Space Station (ISS)* was launched in 1998. It orbits Earth once every 92 minutes. The *ISS* acts as both a science laboratory and a port for spacecraft from all over the world. Since the first expedition in October 2000, 215 people have traveled to the *ISS*. More than 40 crews have visited it. There are plans for many expeditions in the future.

KEY WORDS

Research has shown that as much as 65 percent of all written material published in English is made up of 300 words. These 300 words cannot be taught using pictures or learned by sounding them out. They must be recognized by sight. This book contains 65 common sight words to help young readers improve their reading fluency and comprehension. This book also teaches young readers several important content words. These words are paired with pictures to aid in learning and improve understanding.

Page	Sight Words First Appearance
4	a, around, Earth, from, in, is, it, moves, the, what
5	are, of, other, part, that, their, they, with
6	almost, as, big, how, same
8	and, made, water
11	does, have, like, look, make, only, sometimes, to
12	found, on, river, runs, through, very
15	first, has, one, some, there, walked
16	he, thought, who
19	any, different, for, kinds, land, life, many, no, under
21	about, do, learn, live, study, we, work

Page	Content Words First Appearance
4	path, planet, Sun
5	dwarf planets, objects, space
6	solar system, Venus
8	crust, ice, rocks, surface
11	Blue Planet, oceans
12	Arizona, Grand Canyon, groove
15	astronauts, moon, person
16	Copernicus
21	space station, vehicle

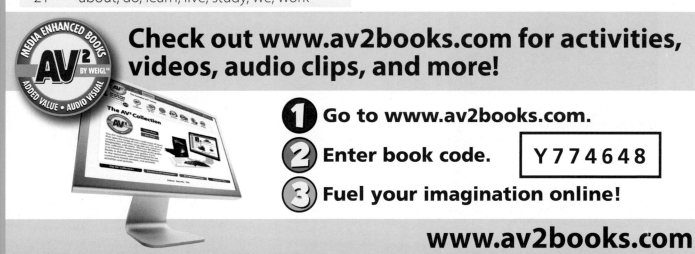

Check out www.av2books.com for activities, videos, audio clips, and more!

1 Go to www.av2books.com.

2 Enter book code. Y 7 7 4 6 4 8

3 Fuel your imagination online!

www.av2books.com